To

_____

From

_____

SMILES for MOM

The quoted ideas expressed in this book (but not scripture verses) are not, in all cases, exact quotations, as some have been edited for clarity and brevity. In all cases, the author has attempted to maintain the speaker's original intent. In some cases, quoted material for this book was obtained from secondary sources, primarily print media. While every effort was made to ensure the accuracy of these sources, the accuracy cannot be guaranteed. For additions, deletions, corrections or clarifications in future editions of this text, please write WALNUT GROVE PRESS.

Scripture quotations are taken from:

The Holy Bible, King James Version

The Holy Bible, New International Version (NIV) Copyright © 1973, 1978, 1984, by International Bible Society. Used by permission of Zondervan Publishing House. All rights reserved.

The Holy Bible, New King James Version (NKJV) Copyright © 1982 by Thomas Nelson, Inc. Used by permission.

The New American Standard Bible®, (NASB) Copyright © 1960, 1962, 1963, 1968, 1971, 1972, 1973, 1975, 1977, 1995 by The Lockman Foundation. Used by permission.

Holy Bible, New Living Translation, (NLT)copyright © 1996. Used by permission of Tyndale House Publishers, Inc., Wheaton, Illinois 60189. All rights reserved.

The Message (MSG)- This edition issued by contractual arrangement with NavPress, a division of The Navigators, U.S.A. Originally published by NavPress in English as THE MESSAGE: The Bible in Contemporary Language copyright 2002-2003 by Eugene Peterson. All rights reserved.

New Century Version®. (NCV) Copyright © 1987, 1988, 1991 by Word Publishing, a division of Thomas Nelson, Inc. All rights reserved. Used by permission.

The Holman Christian Standard Bible™ (HCSB) Copyright © 1999, 2000, 2001 by Holman Bible Publishers. Used by permission.

Cover Design by Kim Russell / Wahoo Designs
Page Layout by Bart Dawson

ISBN 1-58334-262-1

Printed in the United States of America

SMILES
for MOM

second edition

TABLE OF CONTENTS

INTRODUCTION:
A MESSAGE
TO MOTHERS

Few things in life can compare with a mother's love *or* a mother's smile. And, because your Heavenly Father has smiled *upon you* by giving you an earthly family to care for, you have many reasons to be happy. But as you know, being a responsible mom in a demanding world is not always a cause for boundless celebration. Sometimes, being a fully involved parent is tough work—and this book is intended to help.

This book is intended to make you smile *and* to make you think. It contains Bible verses, quotations from noted Christian thinkers, and brief essays—all of which can lift your spirits and guide your path.

So, if God has blessed you with a close-knit clan, smile. After all, God has already smiled upon you. In response, it's your obligation to share His Good News with your family—and with a world—that desperately needs to hear God's message *from you.*

Smiles for Mom

SMILES FOR MOM

Her children rise up and call her blessed.

PROVERBS 31:28 NKJV

Smiles for Mom

BEING A FULL-TIME MOM
IS THE HARDEST JOB
I'VE EVER HAD,
BUT IT IS ALSO
THE BEST JOB
I'VE EVER HAD.
THE PAY IS LOUSY,
BUT THE REWARDS
ARE ETERNAL.

—

Lisa Whelchel

Who deserves a smile more than Mom? Nobody!

Mothers give life and they teach life. They care for us when we're sick and they love us when we deserve it—and when we don't. Our mothers never stop sharing or caring. Yes, our mothers have earned all the good and beautiful things that this world holds, including our smiles. But, mothers also deserve a peace that is beyond the limitations of this earth. That peace is God's peace.

> . . . do not forsake your mother's teaching.
>
> PROVERBS 1:8 NIV

This book is intended to make mothers smile. But it is also intended to remind readers that God, through His Son, Jesus, is the ultimate source of joy and salvation. We are able to smile—today and throughout eternity—because God first smiled upon us. And now, it's our turn to share God's smile with a world that desperately needs His healing grace and His miraculous love.

The mother is and must be,
whether she knows it or not, the greatest, strongest,
and most lasting teacher her children have.

HANNAH WHITALL SMITH

As a mother, my job is to take care of
the possible and trust God with the impossible.

RUTH BELL GRAHAM

Children desperately need to know and hear
in ways they understand and remember
that they're loved and valued by Mom and Dad.

GARY SMALLEY & JOHN TRENT

Children are not so different from kites.
Children were created to fly. But, they need wind,
the undergirding, and strength that comes from
unconditional love, encouragement, and prayer.

GIGI GRAHAM TCHIVIDJIAN

Perfect parents don't exist, but a perfect God does.

BETH MOORE

If you were blessed with a good mother,
you will reap the benefits all of your days.

CHARLES SWINDOLL

"Suzanne will not be at school today,"
I once wrote to her teacher.
"She stayed at home to play with her mother."
I don't remember many other days
of her elementary years. But, I remember that day.

GLORIA GAITHER

Mothers must model the tenderness we need.
Our world can't find it anywhere else.

CHARLES SWINDOLL

Kids go where there is excitement.
They stay where there is love.

ZIG ZIGLAR

Let us look upon our children;
let us love them and train them as children
of the covenant and children of the promise.
These are the children of God.

ANDREW MURRAY

A good woman is the best thing on earth . . . .
The church owes a debt to our faithful women
which we can never estimate, to say nothing of
the debt we owe in our homes to
our godly wives and mothers.

VANCE HAVNER

A person who has a praying mother has
a most cherished possession.

BILLY GRAHAM

For three years, I felt like all I did was pick up toys,
coordinate naps, and kiss boo-boos.
But I began to realize that there was a whole
other level to my life and that I'd never had
a more important job: I was teaching my children
how to respond to God.

LISA WHELCHEL

The children taught me much as they were
growing up: about themselves,
about the world around them, about me,
and especially about God.

RUTH BELL GRAHAM

Let's admit it, we parents make mistakes
in judgement, understanding, and behavior.
There are times when we need to ask forgiveness
from our children.

CATHERINE MARSHALL

I would rather be a nobody in the world,
but be a somebody to my kids.

PATRICK MORLEY

THERE IS NOTHING
MORE SPECIAL,
MORE PRECIOUS THAN
TIME THAT A PARENT
SPENDS STRUGGLING
AND PONDERING
WITH GOD ON BEHALF
OF A CHILD.

MAX LUCADO

It's funny how I am often more comforted
when I find another mom as frazzled as I am
than when I run into an apparent Supermom.
I use the word apparent because there is not a parent
that is a true Supermom; it is merely an apparition.

LISA WHELCHEL

Parents need to make a concerted effort to
build bridges to their kids, starting very early to
have fun as a family, laughing and talking and
doing things that bond the generations together.

JAMES DOBSON

God loves your children through you,
but if you're not available, how can he love them?

JOSH MCDOWELL

From the time I was a very small girl,
I knew that my mother and daddy loved each other.
It was obvious.

GIGI GRAHAM TCHIVIDJIAN

The godly walk with integrity;
blessed are their children after them.

—

PROVERBS 20:7 NLT

A MOTHER'S PRAYER

—

Heavenly Father, help me to be a responsible,
loving, godly mother. Let me teach my children
to worship You and to study Your Holy Word.
When I am uncertain, Lord, give me wisdom.
And, in everything that I do and say,
let me be a worthy example to my family
every day that I live.
Amen

LIFE'S CELEBRATION

Celebrate God all day, every day.
I mean, revel in him!

PHILIPPIANS 4:4 MSG

WE WILL NEVER
BE HAPPY UNTIL
WE MAKE GOD
THE SOURCE OF
OUR FULFILLMENT AND
THE ANSWER
TO OUR LONGINGS.

—

STORMIE OMARTIAN

The 100th Psalm reminds us that the entire earth should "Shout for joy to the LORD" (NIV). As God's children, we are blessed beyond measure, but sometimes, as busy mothers living in a demanding world, we are slow to count our gifts and even slower to give thanks to the Giver.

Our blessings include faith, life, and family—for starters. And, the gifts we receive from God are multiplied when we share them. May we always give thanks to the Creator for His blessings, and may we always demonstrate our gratitude by sharing our gifts with others.

> Rejoice always;
> pray without ceasing.
>
> 2 THESSALONIANS 5:16-17 NASB

The 118th Psalm reminds us that, "This is the day which the LORD has made; let us rejoice and be glad in it" (v. 24, NASB). May we celebrate this day *and* the One who created it.

Christ is the secret, the source, the substance,
the center, and the circumference
of all true and lasting gladness.

MRS. CHARLES E. COWMAN

Whoever possesses God is happy.

ST. AUGUSTINE

When we are set free from the bondage of
pleasing others, when we are free from currying
others' favor and others' approval—then no one
will be able to make us miserable or dissatisfied.
And then, if we know we have pleased God,
contentment will be our consolation.

KAY ARTHUR

Our thoughts, not our circumstances,
determine our happiness.

JOHN MAXWELL

The happiest people in the world are not those
who have no problems, but the people
who have learned to live with those things
that are less than perfect.

JAMES DOBSON

Those who are God's without reserve are,
in every sense, content.

HANNAH WHITALL SMITH

True happiness and contentment cannot come
from the things of this world.
The blessedness of true joy is a free gift that comes
only from our Lord and Savior, Jesus Christ.

DENNIS SWANBERG

We act as though comfort and luxury were the chief
requirements of life, when all we need to make us
really happy is something to be enthusiastic about.

CHARLES KINGSLEY

Father and Mother lived on the edge of poverty,
and yet their contentment was not dependent upon
their surroundings. Their relationship to each other
and to the Lord gave them strength and happiness.

CORRIE TEN BOOM

The happiness which brings enduring worth to life is
not the superficial happiness that is dependent
on circumstances. It is the happiness and
contentment that fills the soul in the midst of
the most distressing of circumstances.

BILLY GRAHAM

Smile—it increases your face value.

ANONYMOUS

When the dream of our heart is one that God has
planted there, a strange happiness flows into us.
At that moment, all of the spiritual resources of
the universe are released to help us.
Our praying is then at one with the will of God and
becomes a channel for the Creator's purposes
for us and our world.

CATHERINE MARSHALL

God designed the human machine to run on
Himself. He Himself is the fuel our spirits
were designed to burn, or the food our spirits
were designed to feed on. There is no other.
That is why it is just no good asking God to make us
happy in our own way without bothering
about religion. God cannot give us a happiness and
peace apart from Himself, because it is not there.
There is no such thing.

C. S. LEWIS

One of the great joys of the great Father's heart is
to make his children glad.

C. H. SPURGEON

IF YOU WANT TO BE
TRULY HAPPY,
YOU WON'T FIND IT ON
AN ENDLESS QUEST
FOR MORE STUFF.
YOU'LL FIND IT IN
RECEIVING GOD'S
GENEROSITY AND
IN PASSING THAT
GENEROSITY ALONG.

BILL HYBELS

God is good, and heaven is forever.
And if those two facts don't cheer you up,
nothing will.

MARIE T. FREEMAN

God has a course mapped out for your life,
and all the inadequacies in the world will not
change His mind. He will be with you every step
of the way. And though it may take time,
He has a celebration planned for when you
cross over the "Red Seas" of your life.

CHARLES SWINDOLL

In terms of the parable of the Prodigal Son,
repentance is the flight home that leads to
joyful celebration. It opens the way to a future,
to a relationship restored.

PHILIP YANCEY

God made round faces; man makes 'em long.

ANONYMOUS

*David and the whole house of Israel were celebrating
with all their might before the LORD,
with songs and with harps, lyres, tambourines,
sistrums and cymbals.*

—

2 SAMUEL 6:5 NIV

A MOTHER'S PRAYER

—

Dear Lord, today, I will join in the celebration
of life. I will be a joyful Christian, and I will share
my joy with all those who cross my path.
You have given me countless blessings, Lord,
and today I will thank You by celebrating my life,
my faith, and my Savior.
Amen

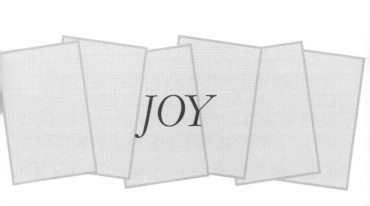

JOY

So now we can rejoice in our wonderful new relationship
with God—all because of what our Lord Jesus Christ
has done for us in making us friends of God.

———

ROMANS 5:11 NLT

AS I CONTEMPLATE ALL
THE SACRIFICES REQUIRED
IN ORDER TO LIVE A LIFE
THAT IS TOTALLY FOCUSED
ON JESUS CHRIST AND
HIS ETERNAL KINGDOM,
THE JOY SEEPS OUT OF
MY HEART ONTO
MY FACE IN A SMILE OF
DEEP SATISFACTION.

—

ANNE GRAHAM LOTZ

Are you a mom whose smile is evident for all to see? If so, congratulations: your joyful spirit serves as a powerful example to your family and friends. And because of your attitude, you may be assured that your children will indeed "rise up" and call you blessed (Proverbs 31:28).

> I will thank the LORD with all my heart; I will declare all Your wonderful works. I will rejoice and boast about You; I will sing about Your name, Most High.
>
> PSALM 9:1-2 HCSB

Sometimes, amid the inevitable hustle and bustle of life here on earth, you may forfeit—albeit temporarily—the joy that God intends for you to experience and to share. But even on life's most difficult days, you may rest assured that God is in His heaven, and He still cares for you.

God's plan for you and your family includes heaping helpings of abundance and joy. Claim them. And remember that Christ offers you and your family priceless gifts: His abundance, His peace, and His joy. Accept those gifts and share them freely, just as Christ has freely shared Himself with you.

We all go through pain and sorrow,
but the presence of God, like a warm,
comforting blanket, can shield us and protect us,
and allow the deep inner joy to surface,
even in the most devastating circumstances.

BARBARA JOHNSON

I wanted the deepest part of me to vibrate
with that ancient yet familiar longing,
that desire for something that would
fill and overflow my soul.

JONI EARECKSON TADA

Some of us seem so anxious about avoiding hell
that we forget to celebrate our journey
toward heaven.

PHILIP YANCEY

Joy is the great note all throughout the Bible.

OSWALD CHAMBERS

Our obedience does not make God any bigger or
better than He already is. Anything God commands
of us is so that our joy may be full—the joy of seeing
His glory revealed to us and in us!

BETH MOORE

Claim the joy that is yours. Pray.
And know that your joy is used
by God to reach others.

KAY ARTHUR

I choose joy. I will refuse the temptation to be
cynical; cynicism is the tool of a lazy thinker.
I will refuse to see people as anything less
than human beings, created by God.
I will refuse to see any problem as anything less
than an opportunity to see God.

MAX LUCADO

The Bible instructs—and experience teaches—
that praising God results in our burdens
being lifted and our joys being multiplied.

JIM GALLERY

JOY IS THE KEYNOTE OF
THE CHRISTIAN LIFE.
IT IS NOT SOMETHING
THAT HAPPENS.
IT IS A GIFT,
GIVEN TO US
IN THE COMING
OF CHRIST.

—

ELISABETH ELLIOT

Jesus did not promise to change the circumstances
around us. He promised great peace and
pure joy to those who would learn to believe
that God actually controls all things.

CORRIE TEN BOOM

I approach prayer in a similar way as I experience
the joy of relationship with God. No matter how
severe "the winter of the soul" may have been,
standing in the presence of God brings pure joy.

HENRY BLACKABY

As Catherine of Siena said, "All the way to heaven
is heaven." A joyful end requires a joyful means.
Bless the Lord.

EUGENE PETERSON

Lord, I thank you for the promise of heaven and
the unexpected moments when you touch
my heartstrings with that longing for
my eternal home.

JONI EARECKSON TADA

Among the most joyful people I have known
have been some who seem to have had
no human reason for joy. The sweet fragrance of
Christ has shown through their lives.

ELISABETH ELLIOT

Joy in life is not the absence of sorrow.
The fact that Jesus could have joy in the midst of
sorrow is proof that we can experience this too.

WARREN WIERSBE

Gratitude changes the pangs of memory
into a tranquil joy.

DIETRICH BONHOEFFER

Will you, with a glad and eager surrender,
hand yourself and all that concerns you over into
his hands? If you will do this, your soul will begin to
know something of the joy of union with Christ.

HANNAH WHITALL SMITH

WHEN I MET CHRIST, I FELT THAT I HAD SWALLOWED SUNSHINE.

—

E. STANLEY JONES

IF YOU'RE A THINKING CHRISTIAN, YOU WILL BE A JOYFUL CHRISTIAN.

—

MARIE T. FREEMAN

Each day, each moment is so pregnant
with eternity that if we "tune in" to it,
we can hardly contain the joy.

GLORIA GAITHER

God knows everything. He can manage everything,
and He loves us. Surely this is enough
for a fullness of joy that is beyond words.

HANNAH WHITALL SMITH

Rejoice, the Lord is King;
Your Lord and King adore!
Rejoice, give thanks and sing
and triumph evermore.

CHARLES WESLEY

Joy is a choice. Joy is a matter of attitude
that stems from one's confidence in God.

CHARLES SWINDOLL

Christ still asks for total surrender and
then promises His gift of full, overflowing joy.

CATHERINE MARSHALL

Shout for joy to the LORD, all the earth.
Worship the LORD with gladness;
come before him with joyful songs.

—

PSALM 100:1-2 NIV

A MOTHER'S PRAYER

———

Dear Lord, You have blessed me
with a loving family—make me a mother
who is thankful, loving, responsible, and wise.
I praise You, Father, for the gift of Your Son and
for the gift of salvation. Let me be a joyful Christian
and a worthy example, this day and
every day that I live.
Amen

SERVANTHOOD

But he who is greatest among you shall be your servant.

—

MATTHEW 23:11 NKJV

I HAVE DISCOVERED THAT
WHEN I PLEASE CHRIST,
I END UP INADVERTENTLY
SERVING OTHERS
FAR MORE EFFECTIVELY.

—

BETH MOORE

Martha and Mary were sisters who both loved Jesus, but they showed their love in different ways. Mary sat at the Master's feet, taking in every word. Martha, meanwhile, busied herself with preparations for the meal to come. When Martha asked Jesus if He was concerned about Mary's failure to help, Jesus replied, "Mary has chosen better" (Luke 10:42 NIV). The implication is clear: as believers, we must spend time *with* Jesus before we spend time *for* him. But, once we have placed Christ where He belongs—at the center of our hearts—we must go about the business of serving the One who has saved us.

How can we serve Christ? By sharing His message, His mercy, and His love with those who cross our paths. Everywhere we look, it seems, the needs are great. Still, our challenge is clear: we must love God, obey His commandments, trust His Son, and serve His children. When we do, we claim spiritual treasures that will endure forever.

> Don't be obsessed with getting your own advantage. Forget yourselves long enough to lend a helping hand.
>
> PHILIPPIANS 2:4 MSG

In the very place where God has put us,
whatever its limitations, whatever kind of work
it may be, we may indeed serve the Lord Christ.

ELISABETH ELLIOT

You can judge how far you have risen
in the scale of life by asking one question:
How wisely and how deeply do I care?
To be Christianized is to be sensitized.
Christians are people who care.

E. STANLEY JONES

Helpfulness means, initially, simple assistance
in trifling, external matters. There is a multitude of
these things wherever people live together.
Nobody is too good for the meanest service.
One who worries about the loss of time
that such petty, outward acts of helpfulness
entail is usually taking the importance of
his own career too solemnly.

DIETRICH BONHOEFFER

Jesus never asks us to give Him what we don't have.
But He does demand that we give Him
all we do have if we want to be a part of what
He wishes to do in the lives of those around us!

ANNE GRAHAM LOTZ

In God's family, there is to be
one great body of people: servants.
In fact, that's the way to the top in his kingdom.

CHARLES SWINDOLL

God wants us to serve Him with a willing spirit,
one that would choose no other way.

BETH MOORE

In the great orchestra we call life,
you have an instrument and a song,
and you owe it to God to play them both sublimely.

MAX LUCADO

So many times we say that we can't serve God
because we aren't whatever is needed.
We're not talented enough or smart enough or
whatever. But if you are in covenant with
Jesus Christ, He is responsible for covering
your weaknesses, for being your strength.
He will give you His abilities for your disabilities!

KAY ARTHUR

We hurt people by being too busy,
too busy to notice their needs.

BILLY GRAHAM

Without God, we cannot.
Without us, God will not.

ST. AUGUSTINE

It is one of the most beautiful compensations of life
that no one can sincerely try
to help another without helping herself.

BARBARA JOHNSON

Unless our belief in God causes us to help
our fellowmen, our faith stands condemned.

BILLY GRAHAM

Employ whatever God has entrusted you with,
in doing good, all possible good,
in every possible kind and degree.

JOHN WESLEY

God has lots of folks who intend to go to work
for him "some day." What He needs is more people
who are willing to work for Him *today*.

MARIE T. FREEMAN

A Christian is a perfectly free lord of all,
subject to none. A Christian is a perfectly
dutiful servant of all, subject to all.

MARTIN LUTHER

God does not do anything with us, only through us.

OSWALD CHAMBERS

When you're enjoying the fulfillment and fellowship
that inevitably accompanies authentic service,
ministry is a joy. Instead of exhausting you,
it energizes you; instead of burnout,
you experience blessing.

BILL HYBELS

Opportunities for service abound, and you will be
surprised that when you seek God's direction,
a place of suitable service will emerge
where you can express your love through service.

CHARLES STANLEY

We are only fully alive when we're helping others.

RICK WARREN

It is common to think that activity in the service
of Christ is the indication of the blessing of God,
but be aware of barrenness in a busy life.

FRANKLIN GRAHAM

That's what I love about serving God.
In His eyes, there are no little people . . .
because there are no big people.
We are all on the same playing field.

JONI EARECKSON TADA

Holy service in constant fellowship
with God is heaven below.

C. H. SPURGEON

Most people want to serve God—
but only in an advisory capacity.

ANONYMOUS

There are times when we are called to love,
expecting nothing in return.
There are times when we are called to give money
to people who will never say thanks,
to forgive those who won't forgive us, to come early
and stay late when no one else notices.

MAX LUCADO

*Think of yourselves the way Christ Jesus
thought of himself. He had equal status with God
but didn't think so much of himself that he had
to cling to the advantages of that status no matter what.
Not at all. When the time came, he set aside
the privileges of deity and took on the status of a slave,
became human! Having become human, he stayed
human. It was an incredibly humbling process.
He didn't claim special privileges. Instead he lived
a selfless, obedient life and he died a selfless,
obedient death, and the worst kind of death at that:
a crucifixion.*

—

PHILIPPIANS 2:5-8 MSG

A MOTHER'S PRAYER

—

Dear Lord, as a mother, I am an example to every
member of my family. Give me a servant's heart
and make me a faithful steward of my gifts. Let me
follow in the footsteps of Your Son Jesus who taught
us by example that to be great in Your eyes, Lord,
is to serve others humbly, faithfully, and lovingly.
Amen

PRAISE AND WORSHIP

I am always praising you; all day long I honor you.

—

PSALM 71:8 NCV

IT'S OUR PRIVILEGE TO
NOT ONLY RAISE OUR HANDS
IN WORSHIP BUT ALSO
TO COMBINE THE VISIBLE
WITH THE INVISIBLE IN
A RISING STREAM OF PRAISE
AND ADORATION SENT
DIRECTLY TO OUR FATHER.

—

SHIRLEY DOBSON

Too many of us, even well-intentioned believers, tend to "compartmentalize" our waking hours into a few familiar categories: work, rest, play, family time, and worship. As creatures of habit, we may find ourselves praising God only at particular times of the day or the week. But praise for our Creator should never be reserved for mealtimes or bedtimes or church. Instead, we should praise God all day, every day, to the greatest extent we can, with thanksgiving in our hearts, and with a song on our lips.

Worship and praise should be woven into the fabric of everything we do; they should not be relegated to a weekly three-hour visit to church on Sunday morning. A. W. Tozer correctly observed,

> Great is the LORD! He is most worthy of praise! His greatness is beyond discovery!
>
> PSALM 145:3 NLT

"If you will not worship God seven days a week, you do not worship Him on one day a week."

Today, find a little more time to lift your prayers to God, and thank Him for all that He has done. Every time you notice a gift from the Giver of all things good, praise Him. His works are marvelous, His gifts are beyond understanding, and His love endures forever.

Nothing we do is more powerful or
more life-changing than praising God.

STORMIE OMARTIAN

Two wings are necessary to lift our souls
toward God: prayer and praise. Prayer asks.
Praise accepts the answer.

MRS. CHARLES E. COWMAN

What happens when we praise the Father?
We reestablish the proper chain of command.

MAX LUCADO

Be not afraid of saying too much in
the praises of God;
all the danger is of saying too little.

MATTHEW HENRY

The best moment to praise God is
always the present one.

MARIE T. FREEMAN

Preoccupy my thoughts with your praise
beginning today.

JONI EARECKSON TADA

The Bible instructs—and experience teaches—
that praising God results in our burdens being lifted
and our joys being multiplied.

JIM GALLERY

How delightful a teacher, but gentle a provider,
how bountiful a giver is my Father!
Praise, praise to Thee, O manifested Most High.

JIM ELLIOT

The time for universal praise is sure to come
some day. Let us begin to do our part now.

HANNAH WHITALL SMITH

Praise Him! Praise Him!
Tell of His excellent greatness;
Praise Him! Praise Him! Ever in joyful song!

FANNY CROSBY

I am to praise God for all things,
regardless of where they seem to originate.
Doing this is the key to receiving
the blessings of God.
Praise will wash away my resentments.

CATHERINE MARSHALL

Praise and thank God for who He is and
for what He has done for you.

BILLY GRAHAM

To worship Him in truth means to worship Him
honestly, without hypocrisy,
standing open and transparent before Him.

ANNE GRAHAM LOTZ

God shows unbridled delight when He sees people
acting in ways that honor Him: when He receives
worship, when He sees faith demonstrated in
the most trying of circumstances, and when He sees
tender love shared among His people.

BILL HYBELS

SPIRITUAL WORSHIP
COMES FROM OUR
VERY CORE AND
IS FUELED BY
AN AWESOME REVERENCE
AND DESIRE FOR GOD.

—

BETH MOORE

God asks that we worship Him
with our concentrated minds as well as
with our wills and emotions.
A divided and scattered mind is not effective.

CATHERINE MARSHALL

Worship is spiritual. Our worship must be
more than just outward expression,
it must also take place in our spirits.

FRANKLIN GRAHAM

It is impossible to worship God and
remain unchanged.

HENRY BLACKABY

In Biblical worship you do not find the repetition of
a phrase; instead, you find the worshipers rehearsing
the character of God and His ways, reminding Him
of His faithfulness and His wonderful promises.

KAY ARTHUR

God actually delights in and pursues our worship
(Proverbs 15:8 & John 4:23).

SHIRLEY DOBSON

It's the definition of worship: A hungry heart finding
the Father's feast. A searching soul finding
the Father's face. A wandering pilgrim spotting
the Father's house. Finding God.
Finding God seeking us. This is worship.
This is a worshiper.

MAX LUCADO

The most common mistake Christians make
in worship today is seeking an experience
rather than seeking God.

RICK WARREN

Worship and worry cannot live in the same heart;
they are mutually exclusive.

RUTH BELL GRAHAM

God is sheer being itself—Spirit.
Those who worship him must do it
out of their very being, their spirits,
their true selves, in adoration.

—

JOHN 4:24 MSG

A MOTHER'S PRAYER

—

When I worship You, Dear Lord, You set my path—
and my heart—straight. Let this day and every day
be a time of worship. Whether I am in Your house or
simply going about my daily activities,
let me worship You, not only with words and deeds,
but also with my heart. In the quiet moments of
the day, I will praise You for creating me,
loving me, guiding me, and saving me.
Amen

PEACE

*Blessed are the peacemakers,
for they shall be called sons of God.*

MATTHEW 5:9 NKJV

GOD CANNOT GIVE US
HAPPINESS AND PEACE APART
FROM HIMSELF, BECAUSE
IT IS NOT THERE. THERE IS
NO SUCH THING.

—

C. S. LEWIS

AND THE PEACE OF GOD,
WHICH TRANSCENDS
ALL UNDERSTANDING,
WILL GUARD YOUR HEARTS AND
YOUR MINDS IN CHRIST JESUS.

—

PHILIPPIANS 4:7 NIV

The beautiful words of John 14:27 give us hope: "Peace I leave with you, my peace I give unto you . . . ." Jesus offers us peace, not as the world gives, but as He alone gives. We, as believers, can accept His peace or ignore it.

When we accept the peace of Jesus Christ into our hearts, our lives are transformed. And then, because we possess the gift of peace, we can share that gift with family members, friends, and fellow believers. If, on the other hand, we choose to ignore the gift of peace—for whatever reason—we cannot share it with others.

For busy mothers, a moment's peace can be a scarce commodity. But no matter how numerous the interruptions and demands of the day, God is ever-present, always ready and willing to offer comfort to those who seek "the peace that passes all understanding." How can we find the peace that we so desperately desire? By turning our days and our lives over to God. Elisabeth Elliot writes, "If my life is surrendered to God, all is well. Let me not grab it back, as though it were in peril in His hand but would be safer in mine!" May we, too, give our lives, our hopes, and our prayers to the Lord, and, by doing so, accept His will and His peace.

Jesus gives us the ultimate rest,
the confidence we need, to escape the frustration
and chaos of the world around us.

BILLY GRAHAM

To know God as He really is—
in His essential nature and character—
is to arrive at a citadel of peace that circumstances
may storm, but can never capture.

CATHERINE MARSHALL

Look around you and you'll be distressed;
look within yourself and you'll be depressed;
look at Jesus, and you'll be at rest!

CORRIE TEN BOOM

God has promised us abundance, peace,
and eternal life. These treasures are ours for
the asking; all we must do is claim them.
One of the great mysteries of life is why on earth
do so many of us wait so very long to claim them?

MARIE T. FREEMAN

PRAYER GUARDS HEARTS AND MINDS AND CAUSES GOD TO BRING PEACE OUT OF CHAOS.

—

BETH MOORE

WE MUST LEARN TO MOVE ACCORDING TO THE TIMETABLE OF THE TIMELESS ONE, AND TO BE AT PEACE.

ELISABETH ELLIOT

A great many people are trying to make peace,
but that has already been done. God has not left it
for us to do; all we have to do is to enter into it.

D. L. MOODY

When peace like a river attendeth my way,
When sorrows like sea billows roll;
Whatever my lot, Thou hast taught me to say,
"It is well, it is well with my soul."

HORATIO G. SPAFFORD

Christ is not only a remedy for your weariness and
trouble, but he will give you an abundance of
the contrary: joy and delight. They who come to
Christ do not only come to a resting-place after they
have been wandering in a wilderness, but they come
to a banqueting-house where they may rest, and
where they may feast. They may cease from their
former troubles and toils, and they may enter
upon a course of delights and spiritual joys.

JONATHAN EDWARDS

There may be no trumpet sound or loud applause
when we make a right decision,
just a calm sense of resolution and peace.

GLORIA GAITHER

What peace can they have
who are not at peace with God?

MATTHEW HENRY

Jesus did not promise to change the circumstances
around us. He promised great peace and pure joy
to those who would learn to believe
that God actually controls all things.

CORRIE TEN BOOM

Believe and do what God says.
The life-changing consequences will be limitless,
and the results will be confidence
and peace of mind.

FRANKLIN GRAHAM

The more closely you cling to the Lord Jesus,
the more clear will your peace be.

C. H. SPURGEON

Rejoicing is a matter of obedience to God—
an obedience that will start you on
the road to peace and contentment.

KAY ARTHUR

Peace with God is where all peace begins.

JIM GALLERY

Let's please God by actively seeking, through prayer,
"peaceful and quiet lives" for ourselves, our spouses,
our children and grandchildren, our friends,
and our nation (1 Timothy 2:1-3 NIV).

SHIRLEY DOBSON

No Jesus, no peace; know Jesus, know peace!

ANONYMOUS

O God, Thou hast made us for Thyself,
and our hearts are restless
until they find their rest in Thee.

ST. AUGUSTINE

Our Father, we are beginning to understand
at last that the things that are wrong with our world
are the sum total of all the things that are wrong
with us as individuals. Thou hast made us after
Thine image, and our hearts can find
no rest until they rest in Thee.

PETER MARSHALL

When something robs you of your peace of mind,
ask yourself if it is worth the energy you are
expending on it. If not, then put it out of
your mind in an act of discipline.
Every time the thought of "it" returns, refuse it.

KAY ARTHUR

Peace does not mean to be in a place
where there is no noise, trouble, or hard work.
Peace means to be in the midst of all those things
and still be calm in your heart.

CATHERINE MARSHALL

When you and I are related to Jesus Christ,
our strength and wisdom and peace and joy and
love and hope may run out, but His life rushes
in to keep us filled to the brim. We are showered
with blessings, not because of anything we have or
have not done, but simply because of Him.

ANNE GRAHAM LOTZ

God's peace is like a river, not a pond.
In other words, a sense of health and well-being,
both of which are expressions of
the Hebrew shalom, can permeate our homes
even when we're in white-water rapids.

BETH MOORE

There is a vital difference between "pacifist" and
"peacemaker." Occasionally the peacemaker has to
whip the daylights out of the troublemakers in order
to have peace. And Jesus never said, "Blessed are
the pacifists" but "Blessed are the peacemakers."

RUTH BELL GRAHAM

I have told you these things,
so that in me you may have peace.
In this world you will have trouble.
But take heart! I have overcome the world.

JOHN 16:33 NIV

A MOTHER'S PRAYER

The world talks about peace, but only You, Lord,
can give a perfect and lasting peace.
True peace comes through the Prince of Peace,
and sometimes His peace passes all understanding.
Help me to accept His peace—and share it—
this day and forever.
Amen

PATIENCE

Those who wait upon the LORD,
they shall inherit the earth.

—

PSALM 37:9 KJV

WHEN I AM DEALING
WITH AN ALL-POWERFUL,
ALL-KNOWING GOD,
I, AS A MERE MORTAL,
MUST OFFER MY
PETITIONS NOT ONLY
WITH PERSISTENCE, BUT
ALSO WITH PATIENCE.
SOMEDAY I'LL KNOW WHY.

—

RUTH BELL GRAHAM

The rigors of motherhood can test the patience of the most even-tempered moms: From time to time, even the most mannerly children may do things that worry us or confuse us or anger us. Why? Because they are children, and because they are human.

As loving parents, we must be patient with our children's shortcomings (just as they, too, must be patient with our own). But our patience must not be restricted to those who live under our care. We must also strive, to the best of our abilities, to exercise patience in all our dealings, because our children are watching and learning.

> Be still before the LORD and wait patiently for Him.
>
> PSALM 37:7 NIV

Sometimes, patience is simply the price we pay for being responsible parents, and that's exactly as it should be. After all, think how patient our Heavenly Father has been with us.

We must learn to wait.
There is grace supplied to the one who waits.

MRS. CHARLES E. COWMAN

You can't step in front of God and
not get in trouble.
When He says, "Go three steps," don't go four.

CHARLES STANLEY

The next time you're disappointed,
don't panic and don't give up. Just be patient and
let God remind you he's still in control.

MAX LUCADO

You're in a hurry. God is not. Trust God.

MARIE T. FREEMAN

To wait upon God is the perfection of activity.

OSWALD CHAMBERS

Waiting is the hardest kind of work,
but God knows best,
and we may joyfully leave all in His hands.

LOTTIE MOON

Let me encourage you to continue to wait
with faith. God may not perform a miracle,
but He is trustworthy to touch you and
make you whole where there used to be a hole.

LISA WHELCHEL

In the name of Jesus Christ who was never in
a hurry, we pray, O God, that You will slow us down,
for we know that we live too fast. With all eternity
before us, make us take time to live—time to get
acquainted with You, time to enjoy Your blessing,
and time to know each other.

PETER MARSHALL

Patience is a virtue that carries a lot of wait.

ANONYMOUS

The deepest spiritual lessons are not learned by
His letting us have our way in the end, but by His
making us wait, bearing with us in love and patience
until we are able honestly to pray what He taught
His disciples to pray: Thy will be done.

ELISABETH ELLIOT

Waiting means going about our assigned tasks,
confident that God will provide
the meaning and the conclusions.

EUGENE PETERSON

God freely admits he is holding back his power,
but he restrains himself for our benefit.
For all scoffers who call for direct action from
the heavens, the prophets have ominous advice:
Just wait.

PHILIP YANCEY

God is in no hurry. Compared to the works
of mankind, He is extremely deliberate.
God is not a slave to the human clock.

CHARLES SWINDOLL

The times we find ourselves having to wait on others
may be the perfect opportunities to train ourselves
to wait on the Lord.

JONI EARECKSON TADA

There is no place for faith if we expect God
to fulfill immediately what he promises.

JOHN CALVIN

No matter what we are going through,
no matter how long the waiting for answers,
of one thing we may be sure. God is faithful.
He keeps His promises. What He starts,
He finishes . . . including His perfect work in us.

GLORIA GAITHER

To receive the blessing we need, we must believe
and keep on believing, to wait and keep on waiting.
We need to wait in prayer, wait with our Bibles open
as we confess his promises, wait in joyful praise and
worship of the God who will never forget our case,
and wait as we continue serving others in his name.

JIM CYMBALA

How do you wait upon the Lord?
First you must learn to sit at His feet
and take time to listen to His words.

KAY ARTHUR

*Now it happened as they went that He entered
a certain village; and a certain woman named Martha
welcomed Him into her house. And she had a sister
called Mary, who also sat at Jesus' feet and heard
His word. But Martha was distracted with much
serving, and she approached Him and said, "Lord,
do You not care that my sister has left me to serve alone?
Therefore tell her to help me." And Jesus answered
and said to her, "Martha, Martha, you are worried
and troubled about many things. But one thing
is needed, and Mary has chosen that good part,
which will not be taken away from her."*

LUKE 10:38-42 NKJV

Wait on the Lord, wait patiently,
And thou shalt in Him be blest;
After the storm, a holy calm,
And after thy labor rest.

FANNY CROSBY

When there is perplexity there is always guidance—
not always at the moment we ask,
but in good time, which is God's time.
There is no need to fret and stew.

ELISABETH ELLIOT

If you want to hear God's voice clearly and
you are uncertain, then remain in His presence
until He changes that uncertainty.
Often much can happen during this waiting for
the Lord. Sometimes he changes pride
into humility; doubt into faith and peace . . . .

CORRIE TEN BOOM

Be gentle to all, able to teach, patient.

2 TIMOTHY 2:24 NKJV

A MOTHER'S PRAYER

Lord, make me a mother who has patience.
When I am hurried, give me peace.
When I am frustrated, give me perspective.
When I am angry, let me turn my heart to You.
Today, let me be a patient Christian, Dear Lord,
as I trust in You and in Your master plan for my life.
Amen

WISDOM

Teach me Your way, O Lord;
I will walk in Your truth.

—

PSALM 86:11 NASB

GOD HIMSELF IS WHAT
ENLIGHTENS UNDERSTANDING
ABOUT EVERYTHING ELSE
IN LIFE. KNOWLEDGE ABOUT
ANY SUBJECT IS FRAGMENTARY
WITHOUT
THE ENLIGHTENMENT THAT
COMES FROM
HIS RELATIONSHIP TO IT.

—

BETH MOORE

Do you seek wisdom for yourself and for your family? Of course you do. But as a savvy mom, you know that wisdom can be an elusive commodity in today's troubled world. In a society filled with temptations and distractions, it's easy for parents and children alike to stray far from the source of the ultimate wisdom: God's Holy Word.

When you begin a daily study of God's Word and live according to His commandments, you will become wise . . . in time. But don't expect to open your Bible today and be wise tomorrow. Wisdom is not like a mushroom; it does not spring up overnight. It is, instead, like an oak tree that starts as a tiny acorn, grows into a sapling, and eventually reaches up to the sky, tall and strong.

> But if any of you needs wisdom, you should ask God for it. He is generous and enjoys giving to all people, so he will give you wisdom.
>
> JAMES 1:5 NCV

Today and every day, as a way of understanding God's plan for your life, study His Word and live by it. When you do, you will accumulate a storehouse of wisdom that will enrich your own life and the lives of your family members, your friends, and the world.

Knowledge can be found in books or in school.
Wisdom, on the other hand, starts with God . . .
and ends there.

MARIE T. FREEMAN

This is my song through endless ages:
Jesus led me all the way.

FANNY CROSBY

Don't expect wisdom to come into your life
like great chunks of rock on a conveyor belt.
Wisdom comes privately from God as a byproduct of
right decisions, godly reactions, and the application
of spiritual principles to daily circumstances.

CHARLES SWINDOLL

Most of us go through life praying a little,
planning a little, jockeying for position, hoping
but never being quite certain of anything,
and always secretly afraid that we will miss the way.
This is a tragic waste of truth and never gives rest to
the heart. There is a better way. It is to repudiate
our own wisdom and take instead
the infinite wisdom of God.

A. W. TOZER

When you and I are related to Jesus Christ,
our strength and wisdom and peace and joy and
love and hope may run out, but His life rushes in to
keep us filled to the brim. We are showered
with blessings, not because of anything we have or
have not done, but simply because of Him.

ANNE GRAHAM LOTZ

God's plan for our guidance is for us to grow
gradually in wisdom before we get to the crossroads.

BILL HYBELS

Knowledge is horizontal. Wisdom is vertical;
it comes down from above.

BILLY GRAHAM

Wisdom is knowledge applied.
Head knowledge is useless on the battlefield.
Knowledge stamped on the heart makes one wise.

BETH MOORE

There is a difficulty about disagreeing with God.
He is the source from which all your reasoning
power comes: you could not be right and He wrong
any more than a stream can rise higher than its
own source. When you are arguing against Him
you are arguing against the very power that makes
you able to argue at all: it is like cutting off
the branch you are sitting on.

C. S. LEWIS

The fruit of wisdom is Christlikeness, peace,
humility, and love. And, the root of it is faith in
Christ as the manifested wisdom of God.

J. I. PACKER

We forget that God sometimes has to say "No."
We pray to Him as our heavenly Father,
and like wise human fathers, He often says, "No,"
not from whim or caprice, but from wisdom,
from love, and from knowing what is best for us.

PETER MARSHALL

If you lack knowledge, go to school.
If you lack wisdom, get on your knees.

VANCE HAVNER

With the goodness of God to desire our highest
welfare and the wisdom of God to plan it,
what do we lack?
Surely we are the most favored of all creatures.

A. W. TOZER

Wisdom is the right use of knowledge. To know is
not to be wise. Many men know a great deal,
and are all the greater fools for it. But to know
how to use knowledge is to have wisdom.

C. H. SPURGEON

The essence of wisdom, from a practical standpoint,
is pausing long enough to look at our lives—
invitations, opportunities, relationships—
from God's perspective. And then acting on it.

CHARLES STANLEY

The theme of Proverbs is wisdom,
the right use of knowledge.
It enables you to evaluate circumstances and
people and make the right decisions in life.

WARREN WIERSBE

We will never cease to need our Father—
His wisdom, direction, help, and support.
We will never outgrow Him.
We will always need His grace.

KAY ARTHUR

The more wisdom enters our hearts,
the more we will be able to trust our hearts
in difficult situations.

JOHN ELDREDGE

Christ teaches by the Spirit of wisdom in
the heart, opening the understanding to
the Spirit of revelation in the word.

MATTHEW HENRY

God's guidance is even more important than
common sense. I can declare that the deepest
darkness is outshone by the light of Jesus.

CORRIE TEN BOOM

We are all faced with a series of great opportunities,
brilliantly disguised as unsolvable problems.
Unsolvable without God's wisdom, that is.

CHARLES SWINDOLL

Hold your children before the Lord in fervent prayer
throughout their years at home. There is no other
source of confidence and wisdom in parenting.
The God who made your children will hear
your petitions. He has promised to do so.

JAMES DOBSON

Grace comes from the heart of a gracious God
who wants to stun you and overwhelm you with
a gift you don't deserve—salvation, adoption,
a spiritual ability to use in kingdom service,
answered prayer, the church, His presence,
His wisdom, His guidance, His love.

BILL HYBELS

*Anyone who listens to my teaching and
obeys me is wise, like a person who builds a house
on solid rock. Though the rain comes in torrents and
the floodwaters rise and the winds beat against
that house, it won't collapse, because it is built on rock.*

MATTHEW 7:24–25 NLT

A MOTHER'S PRAYER

Dear Lord, give me wisdom to love my family,
to care for them, and to help them understand
the wisdom of Your Holy Word. Let me share
Your wisdom by the words I speak and the example
that I set, today and every day that I live.
Amen

LAUGHTER

There is a time for everything,
and everything on earth has its special season.
There is a time to cry and a time to laugh . . . .
There is a time to be sad and a time to dance.

ECCLESIASTES 3:1, 4 NCV

LAUGHTER DULLS
THE SHARPEST PAIN AND
FLATTENS OUT
THE GREATEST STRESS.
TO SHARE IT IS TO GIVE
A GIFT OF HEALTH.

—

BARBARA JOHNSON

otherhood is no laughing matter; it should be taken very seriously, up to a point. But no mother's responsibilities should be so burdensome that she forgets to laugh. Laughter is medicine for the soul, but sometimes, amid the stresses of the day, we forget to take our medicine. Instead of viewing our world with a mixture of optimism and humor, we allow worries and distractions to rob us of the joy that God intends for our lives.

If your heart is heavy, open the door of your soul to Christ. He will give you peace and joy. And, if you already have the joy of Christ in your heart, share it freely, just as Christ freely shared His joy with you. As you go about your daily activities, approach life with a smile on your lips and hope in your heart. And laugh every chance you get. After all, God created laughter for a reason . . . and Father indeed knows best. So laugh!

> A happy heart is like good medicine.
>
> PROVERBS 17:22 NCV

There is nothing that rejuvenates the parched,
delicate spirits of children faster than when
a lighthearted spirit pervades the home and
laughter fills its halls.

JAMES DOBSON

I think everybody ought to be a laughing Christian.
I'm convinced that there's just one place
where there's not any laughter, and that's hell.

JERRY CLOWER

He who laughs lasts—he who doesn't, doesn't.

MARIE T. FREEMAN

I want to encourage you in these days with
your family to lighten up and enjoy.
Laugh a little bit; it might just set you free.

DENNIS SWANBERG

It is often just as sacred to laugh as it is to pray.

CHARLES SWINDOLL

A keen sense of humor helps us to
overlook the unbecoming,
understand the unconventional,
tolerate the unpleasant,
overcome the unexpected,
and outlast the unbearable.

BILLY GRAHAM

To have fallen in love hints to our hearts
that all of earthly life is not hopelessly fallen.
Love is the laughter of God.

BETH MOORE

After the forgiving comes laughter, a deeper love—
and further opportunities to forgive.

RUTH BELL GRAHAM

When you have good, healthy relationships
with your family and friends you're more prompted
to laugh and not take yourself so seriously.

DENNIS SWANBERG

Those who are God's without reserve are,
in every sense, content.

HANNAH WHITALL SMITH

Joy is the serious business of heaven.

C. S. LEWIS

Two indications of a person's character are
what makes him laugh and what makes him weep.

WARREN WIERSBE

We can never untangle all the woes in other
people's lives. We can't produce miracles overnight.
But we can bring a cup of cool water to
a thirsty soul, or a scoop of laughter to
a lonely heart.

BARBARA JOHNSON

The next time you hear a baby laugh or
see an ocean wave, take note. Pause and listen
as his Majesty whispers ever so gently, "I'm here."

MAX LUCADO

Laugh until you feel better—
and the devil feels worse!

ANONYMOUS

I am truly happy with Jesus Christ.
I couldn't live without Him.

RUTH BELL GRAHAM

Christ is the secret, the source, the substance,
the center, and the circumference of
all true and lasting gladness.

MRS. CHARLES E. COWMAN

Wherever you are, be all there.
Live to the hilt every situation you believe
to be the will of God.

JIM ELLIOT

Catch on fire with enthusiasm and people
will come for miles to watch you burn.

JOHN WESLEY

Holy activity is the mother of holy joy.

C. H. SPURGEON

Joy is available to all who seek His riches.
The key to joy is found in the person of Jesus Christ
and in His will.

KAY ARTHUR

When we bring sunshine into the lives of others,
we're warmed by it ourselves.
When we spill a little happiness,
it splashes on us.

BARBARA JOHNSON

. . . as the occasion when Jews got relief from their enemies, the month in which their sorrow turned to joy, mourning somersaulted into a holiday for parties and fun and laughter, the sending and receiving of presents and of giving gifts to the poor.

ESTHER 9:22 MSG

A MOTHER'S PRAYER

—

Dear Lord, laughter is Your gift.
Today and every day, put a smile on my face,
and let me share that smile with all
who cross my path, starting with my family.
Amen

FORGIVENESS

*Praise the LORD, I tell myself, and never forget
the good things he does for me.
He forgives all my sins and heals all my diseases.*

—

PSALM 103:3 NLT

LEARNING HOW TO
FORGIVE AND FORGET IS
ONE OF THE SECRETS OF
A HAPPY CHRISTIAN LIFE.

WARREN WIERSBE

E ven the most mild-mannered moms will, on occasion, have reason to become angry with the inevitable shortcomings of family members and friends. But wise women are quick to forgive others, just as God has forgiven them.

Forgiveness is God's commandment, but oh how difficult a commandment it can be to follow. Being frail, fallible, imperfect human beings, we are quick to anger, quick to blame, slow to forgive, and even slower to forget. No matter. Even when forgiveness is difficult, God's Word is clear.

If, in your heart, you hold bitterness against even a single person, forgive. If there exists even one person, alive or dead, whom you have not forgiven, follow God's commandment

> In prayer there is a connection between what God does and what you do. You can't get forgiveness from God, for instance, without also forgiving others. If you refuse to do your part, you cut yourself off from God's part.
>
> MATTHEW 6:14-15 MSG

and His will for your life: forgive. If you are embittered against yourself for some past mistake or shortcoming, forgive. Then, to the best of your abilities, forget, and move on. Bitterness and regret are not part of God's plan for your life. Forgiveness is.

When God forgives, He forgets.
He buries our sins in the sea and puts a sign on
the shore saying, "No Fishing Allowed."

CORRIE TEN BOOM

It doesn't matter how big the sin is or how small;
it doesn't matter whether it was spontaneous
or malicious. God will forgive you
if you come to Him and confess your sin!

ANNE GRAHAM LOTZ

God no longer deals with us in judgment
but in mercy. If people got what they deserved,
this old planet would have ripped apart at
the seams centuries ago.

JONI EARECKSON TADA

Two works of mercy set a man free:
forgive and you will be forgiven,
and give and you will receive.

ST. AUGUSTINE

Forgiveness is actually the best revenge because
it not only sets us free from the person we forgive,
but it frees us to move into all that
God has in store for us.

STORMIE OMARTIAN

Forgiveness is contagious. First you forgive them,
and pretty soon, they'll forgive you, too.

MARIE T. FREEMAN

Our Savior kneels down and gazes upon the darkest
acts of our lives. But rather than recoil in horror,
he reaches out in kindness and says, "I can clean
that if you want." And, from the basin of his grace,
he scoops a palm full of mercy and washes our sin.

MAX LUCADO

An eye for an eye and a tooth for a tooth . . .
and pretty soon, everybody's blind
and wearing dentures.

ANONYMOUS

Forgiveness is not an emotion.
Forgiveness is an act of the will,
and the will can function regardless
of the temperature of the heart.

CORRIE TEN BOOM

Miracles broke the physical laws of the universe;
forgiveness broke the moral rules.

PHILIP YANCEY

To hold on to hate and resentments is
to throw a monkey wrench
into the machinery of life.

E. STANLEY JONES

When you harbor bitterness,
happiness will dock elsewhere.

ANONYMOUS

As you have received the mercy of God
by the forgiveness of sin and the promise
of eternal life, thus you must show mercy.

BILLY GRAHAM

There is no use in talking as if forgiveness were easy.
I could say of a certain man,
"Have I forgiven him more times than I can count?"
For we find that the work of forgiveness
has to be done over and over again.

C. S. LEWIS

Our relationships with other people are of
primary importance to God. Because God is love,
He cannot tolerate any unforgiveness or hardness in
us toward any individual.

CATHERINE MARSHALL

It is said that forgiveness is the fragrance
the violet sheds on the heel that has crushed it.
If so, could there be a fragrance as sweet in all
the Bible as that of Jesus washing the feet of
the very one whose heel was raised against Him?

CHARLES SWINDOLL

We cannot out-sin God's ability to forgive us.

BETH MOORE

If Jesus forgave those who nailed Him to the Cross,
and if God forgives you and me,
how can you withhold your forgiveness
from someone else?

ANNE GRAHAM LOTZ

The well of God's forgiveness never runs dry.

GRADY NUTT

Looking back over my life, all I can see is mercy and
grace written in large letters everywhere.
May God help me have the same kind of heart
toward those who wound or offend me.

JIM CYMBALA

Let's take Jesus at his word.
When he says we're forgiven, let's unload the guilt.
When he says we're valuable, let's believe him.
When he says we're eternal, let's bury our fear.
When he says we're provided for, let's stop worrying.

MAX LUCADO

God specializes in taking bruised, soiled, broken,
guilty, and miserable vessels and making them
whole, forgiven, and useful again.

CHARLES SWINDOLL

Forgiveness is the key that unlocks the door of
resentment and the handcuffs of hate.
It is a power that breaks the chains of bitterness and
the shackles of selfishness.

CORRIE TEN BOOM

Above all, love each other deeply,
because love covers a multitude of sins.

—

1 PETER 4:8 NIV

A MOTHER'S PRAYER

—

Lord, I know that I need to forgive others
just as You have forgiven me. Help me to be
an example of forgiveness to my children.
Keep me mindful, Father, that I am never
fully liberated until I have been freed from
the chains of bitterness—and that You offer me
that freedom through Your Son, Christ Jesus.
Amen

EXAMPLE

In everything set them an example
by doing what is good.

—

TITUS 2:7 NIV

AMONG THE MOST JOYFUL PEOPLE
I HAVE KNOWN HAVE BEEN SOME
WHO SEEM TO HAVE HAD
NO HUMAN REASON FOR JOY.
THE SWEET FRAGRANCE OF CHRIST
HAS SHOWN THROUGH
THEIR LIVES.

—

ELISABETH ELLIOT

WE HAVE AROUND US MANY PEOPLE
WHOSE LIVES TELL US WHAT
FAITH MEANS. SO LET US RUN
THE RACE THAT IS BEFORE US AND
NEVER GIVE UP. WE SHOULD
REMOVE FROM OUR LIVES
ANYTHING THAT WOULD GET
IN THE WAY AND THE SIN
THAT SO EASILY HOLDS US BACK.

—

HEBREWS 12:1 NCV

Our children learn from the lessons we teach and the lives we live, but not necessarily in that order. As mothers, we serve as unforgettable role models for our children and grandchildren. Hopefully, the lives we lead and the choices we make will serve as enduring examples of the spiritual abundance that is available to all who worship God and obey His commandments.

What kind of example are you? Are you the kind of mother whose life serves as a genuine example of patience and righteousness? Are you a woman whose behavior serves as a positive role model for others? Are you the kind of mom whose actions, day in and day out, are based upon kindness, faithfulness, and a sincere love for the Lord? If so, you are not only blessed by God; you are also a powerful force for good in a world that desperately needs positive influences such as yours.

Corrie ten Boom advised, "Don't worry about what you do not understand. Worry about what you do understand in the Bible but do not live by." And that's sound advice because our families and friends are watching . . . and so, for that matter, is God.

The religion of Jesus Christ has an ethical
as well as a doctrinal side.

LOTTIE MOON

In our faith we leave footprints to guide others.
A child, a friend, a recent convert.
None should be left to walk the trail alone.

MAX LUCADO

For one man who can introduce another to
Jesus Christ by the way he lives and by
the atmosphere of his life, there are a thousand
who can only talk jargon about him.

OSWALD CHAMBERS

It's good to be saved and know it!
It's also good to be saved and show it!

ANONYMOUS

There is too much sermonizing and
too little witnessing. People do not come to Christ
at the end of an argument.

VANCE HAVNER

Whether we signed up for the responsibility or not,
Christian parents give their children impressions of
what they can expect from God.

BETH MOORE

We urgently need people who encourage and
inspire us to move toward God and away from
the world's enticing pleasures.

JIM CYMBALA

Is your child learning of the love of God
through your love, tenderness, and mercy?

JAMES DOBSON

Our walk counts far more than our talk, always!

GEORGE MUELLER

Jesus—the standard of measurement,
the scale of weights, the test of character
for the whole moral universe.

R. G. LEE

IF WE HAVE THE TRUE LOVE
OF GOD IN OUR HEARTS,
WE WILL SHOW IT
IN OUR LIVES. WE WILL NOT
HAVE TO GO UP AND DOWN
THE EARTH PROCLAIMING IT.
WE WILL SHOW IT
IN EVERYTHING
WE SAY OR DO.

—

D. L. MOODY

Nothing speaks louder or more powerfully
than a life of integrity.

CHARLES SWINDOLL

Parents can tell but never teach,
until they practice what they preach.

ANONYMOUS

Your light is the truth of the Gospel message
itself as well as your witness as to Who Jesus is and
what He has done for you. Don't hide it.

ANNE GRAHAM LOTZ

You are the light that gives light to the world . . . .
In the same way, you should be a light for
other people. Live so that they will see
the good things you do and will praise
your Father in heaven.

MATTHEW 5:14, 16 NCV

Integrity of heart is indispensable.

JOHN CALVIN

Learning God's truth and getting it into our heads is
one thing, but *living* God's truth and getting it
into our characters is quite something else.

WARREN WIERSBE

Integrity is not a given factor in everyone's life.
It is a result of self-discipline, inner trust,
and a decision to be relentlessly honest
in all situations in our lives.

JOHN MAXWELL

It is the thoughts and intents of the heart
that shape a person's life.

JOHN ELDREDGE

There's nothing like the power of integrity.
It is a characteristic so radiant, so steady,
so consistent, so beautiful, that it makes
a permanent picture in our minds.

FRANKLIN GRAHAM

What lessons about honor did you learn
from your childhood?
Are you living what you learned today?

DENNIS SWANBERG

Integrity is the glue that holds our way
of life together. We must constantly strive
to keep our integrity intact. When wealth is lost,
nothing is lost; when health is lost,
something is lost; when character is lost, all is lost.

BILLY GRAHAM

Character is not something highly valued
in this society, so it is most important that
the development of strong character be emphasized
and rewarded in the home.

CHARLES STANLEY

Integrity is a sign of maturity.

CHARLES SWINDOLL

The integrity of the upright guides them,
but the unfaithful are destroyed by their duplicity.

—

PROVERBS 11:3 NIV

A MOTHER'S PRAYER

—

Dear Lord, help me be a worthy example
to my children, to my family members,
and to my friends. Let the things that I say and
the things that I do show everyone what it means
to be a follower of Your Son.

Amen

Kindness

KINDNESS

And be kind to one another, tenderhearted,
forgiving one another, just as God in Christ forgave you.

—

EPHESIANS 4:32 NKJV

Kindness

KINDNESS IN THIS WORLD
WILL DO MUCH TO HELP
OTHERS, NOT ONLY TO
COME INTO THE LIGHT,
BUT ALSO TO GROW
IN GRACE DAY BY DAY.

—

FANNY CROSBY

In the busyness and confusion of daily life, it is easy to lose focus, and it is easy to become frustrated. We are imperfect human beings struggling to manage our lives as best we can, but we often fall short. When we are distracted or disappointed, we may neglect to share a kind word or a kind deed. This oversight hurts others, but it hurts us most of all.

Kindness is God's commandment. Matthew 25:40 warns, "Whatever you did for one of the least of these brothers of Mine, you did for Me" (HCSB). When we extend the hand of friendship to those who need it most, God promises His blessings. When we ignore the needs of others—or mistreat them—we risk God's retribution.

Today, slow yourself down and be alert for those who need your smile, your kind words, or your helping hand. Make kindness a centerpiece of your dealings with others. They will be blessed, and you will be, too. When you spread a heaping helping of encouragement and hope to the world, you can't help getting a little bit on yourself.

> So, as those who have been chosen of God, holy and beloved, put on a heart of compassion, kindness, humility, gentleness and patience.
>
> COLOSSIANS 3:12 NASB

Here lies the tremendous mystery—that God
should be all-powerful, yet refuse to coerce.
He summons us to cooperation. We are honored in
being given the opportunity to participate in
his good deeds. Remember how He asked for help in
performing his miracles: Fill the water pots,
stretch out your hand, distribute the loaves.

ELISABETH ELLIOT

When you extend hospitality to others,
you're not trying to impress people,
you're trying to reflect God to them.

MAX LUCADO

The mark of a Christian is that he will walk
the second mile and turn the other cheek.
A wise man or woman gives the extra effort,
all for the glory of the Lord Jesus Christ.

JOHN MAXWELL

Be so preoccupied with good will
that you haven't room for ill will.

E. STANLEY JONES

The Golden Rule starts at home,
but it should never stop there.

MARIE T. FREEMAN

Scientists tell us that every word and picture,
every broadcast electronically, is still somewhere
out in space, billions of miles away. If humans ever
go to other planets, they may see an old episode
of "Gunsmoke." Amazing as that sounds, there is
something even more astonishing: Not a single act
of goodness in Jesus' name has ever disappeared.
Every act of kindness reaches out and touches
the lives of thousands of people—one at a time.

DENNIS SWANBERG

If we have the true love of God in our hearts,
we will show it in our lives. We will not have to go
up and down the earth proclaiming it.
We will show it in everything we say or do.

D. L. MOODY

Faith never asks whether good works are to be done,
but has done them before there is time to ask
the question, and it is always doing them.

MARTIN LUTHER

Do all the good you can. By all the means you can.
In all the ways you can. In all the places you can.
At all the times you can. To all the people you can.
As long as you can.

JOHN WESLEY

Discouraged people don't need critics.
They hurt enough already. They don't need more
guilt or piled-on distress. They need encouragement.
They need a refuge, a willing, caring,
available someone.

CHARLES SWINDOLL

A single word, if spoken in a friendly spirit,
may be sufficient to turn one from dangerous error.

FANNY CROSBY

Encouragement is the oxygen of the soul.

JOHN MAXWELL

Make it a rule, and pray to God to help you to keep it, never, if possible, to lie down at night without being able to say: "I have made one human being at least a little wiser, or a little happier, or at least a little better this day."

CHARLES KINGSLEY

I have discovered that when I please Christ, I end up inadvertently serving others far more effectively.

BETH MOORE

There are times when we are called to love, expecting nothing in return. There are times when we are called to give money to people who will never say thanks, to forgive those who won't forgive us, to come early and stay late when no one else notices.

MAX LUCADO

That's what I love about serving God. In His eyes, there are no little people . . . because there are no big people. We are all on the same playing field.

JONI EARECKSON TADA

Service is love in overalls!

ANONYMOUS

We are only fully alive when we're helping others.

RICK WARREN

Before the judgment seat of Christ,
my service will not be judged by how much
I have done but by how much of me there is in it.

A. W. TOZER

You can judge how far you have risen in
the scale of life by asking one question:
How wisely and how deeply do I care?
To be Christianized is to be sensitized.
Christians are people who care.

E. STANLEY JONES

So many times we say that we can't serve God
because we aren't whatever is needed.
We're not talented enough or smart enough or
whatever. But if you are in covenant with
Jesus Christ, He is responsible for covering
your weaknesses, for being your strength.
He will give you His abilities for your disabilities!

KAY ARTHUR

Helpfulness means, initially, simple assistance
in trifling, external matters. There is a multitude of
these things wherever people live together.
Nobody is too good for the meanest service.
One who worries about the loss of time that
such petty, outward acts of helpfulness
entail is usually taking the importance
of his own career too solemnly.

DIETRICH BONHOEFFER

Jesus never asks us to give Him what we don't have.
But He does demand that we give Him
all we do have if we want to be a part of what
He wishes to do in the lives of those around us!

ANNE GRAHAM LOTZ

May the Lord cause you to increase and
abound in love for one another,
and for all people.

—

1 THESSALONIANS 3:12 NASB

A MOTHER'S PRAYER

—

Lord, make me a loving, encouraging
Christian mother. And, let my love for Christ
be reflected through the kindness that I show to
those who need the healing touch of
the Master's hand.
Amen

GOD'S LOVE

His banner over me was love.

—

SONG OF SOLOMON 2:4 KJV

KNOWING
GOD'S SOVEREIGNTY AND
UNCONDITIONAL LOVE
IMPARTS A BEAUTY
TO LIFE . . . AND TO YOU.

—

KAY ARTHUR

As a mother, you know the profound love that you hold in your heart for your own children. As a child of God, you can only imagine the infinite love that your Heavenly Father holds for you.

God made you in His own image and gave you salvation through the person of His Son Jesus Christ. And now, precisely because you are a wondrous creation treasured by God, a question presents itself: What will you do in response to the Creator's love? Will you ignore it or embrace it? Will you return it or neglect it? That decision, of course, is yours and yours alone.

> For I am persuaded that neither death nor life, nor angels nor rulers, nor things present, nor things to come, nor powers, nor height, nor depth, nor any other created thing will have the power to separate us from the love of God that is in Christ Jesus our Lord!
>
> ROMANS 8:38-39 HCSB

When you embrace God's love, you are forever changed. When you embrace God's love, you feel differently about yourself, your neighbors, your family, and your world. More importantly, you share God's message—and His love—with others.

Your Heavenly Father—a God of infinite love and mercy—is waiting to embrace you with open arms. Accept His love today and forever.

Believing that you are loved will set you free
to be who God created you to be.
So rest in His love and just be yourself.

LISA WHELCHEL

The question of whether or not God loves you and
is concerned about you has nothing to do with
the circumstances surrounding you right now.
That question was settled a long time ago.

CHARLES STANLEY

He screens the suffering,
filtering it through fingers of love.

JONI EARECKSON TADA AND STEVE ESTES

Though we may not act like our Father,
there is no greater truth than this: We are his.
Unalterably. He loves us. Undyingly.
Nothing can separate us from the love of Christ.

MAX LUCADO

Jesus loves us with fidelity, purity, constancy,
and passion, no matter how imperfect we are.

STORMIE OMARTIAN

God loves each of us as if there were only one of us.

ST. AUGUSTINE

The spectacle of the Cross, the most public event of
Jesus' life, reveals the vast difference between
a god who proves himself through power and
One who proves himself through love.

PHILIP YANCEY

If you have a true faith that Christ is your Savior,
then at once you have a gracious God, for faith leads
you in and opens up God's heart and will,
that you should see pure grace and overflowing love.

MARTIN LUTHER

God wants to reveal Himself as your heavenly
Father. When you are hurting, you can run to Him
and crawl up into His lap. When you wonder
which way to turn, you can grasp His strong hand,
and He'll guide you along life's path.
When everything around you is falling apart,
you'll feel your Father's arm around your shoulder
to hold you together.

LISA WHELCHEL

The springs of love are in God, not in us.

OSWALD CHAMBERS

Nails didn't hold Jesus on the cross.
His love for you did.

ANONYMOUS

God has pursued us from farther than space and
longer than time.

JOHN ELDREDGE

God loves us the way we are,
but He loves us too much to leave us that way.

LEIGHTON FORD

Snuggle in God's arms. When you are hurting,
when you feel lonely or left out, let Him cradle you,
comfort you, reassure you of His
all-sufficient power and love.

KAY ARTHUR

The fact is, God no longer deals with us in judgment
but in mercy. If people got what they deserved,
this old planet would have ripped apart at the seams
centuries ago. Praise God that because of His great
love "we are not consumed, for his compassions
never fail" (Lam. 3:22).

JONI EARECKSON TADA

Even when we cannot see the why and wherefore of
God's dealings, we know that there is love in
and behind them, so we can rejoice always.

J. I. PACKER

LOVE SO AMAZING,
SO DIVINE,
DEMANDS MY SOUL,
MY LIFE, MY ALL.

—

ISAAC WATTS

The life of faith is a daily exploration of
the constant and countless ways in which
God's grace and love are experienced.

EUGENE PETERSON

Behold, behold the wondrous love,
That ever flows from God above
Through Christ His only Son, Who gave
His precious blood our souls to save.

FANNY CROSBY

Being loved by Him whose opinion matters most
gives us the security to risk loving, too—
even loving ourselves.

GLORIA GAITHER

To be loved by God is the highest relationship,
the highest achievement,
and the highest position of life.

HENRY BLACKABY AND CLAUDE KING

*Unfailing love surrounds those who trust the L*ORD.

—

PSALM 32:10 NLT

A MOTHER'S PRAYER

—

Lord, Your love is infinite and eternal.
Although I cannot fully understand the depths
of Your love, I can praise it, return it,
and share it always. Make my love for others
and my love for You a shining example to my family
and to all whom You place along my path,
today and forever.
Amen

THANKS, MOM!

In everything give thanks;
for this is the will of God in Christ Jesus for you.

—

1 THESSALONIANS 5:18 NKJV

Thanks, Mom!

A SPIRIT OF
THANKFULNESS
MAKES
ALL THE DIFFERENCE.

—

BILLY GRAHAM

We conclude with a message of thanks to marvelous mothers everywhere:

DEAR MOM,

Thanks for the love, the care, the work, the discipline, the wisdom, the support, and the faith. Thanks for being a concerned parent and a worthy example. Thanks for giving life and for teaching it. Thanks for being patient with me, even when you were tired or frustrated—or both. Thanks for changing diapers and wiping away tears. And thanks for being a godly woman, one worthy of our admiration and our love.

> Her children rise up and call her blessed.
>
> PROVERBS 31:28 NKJV

You deserve a smile today, Mom, but you deserve so much more. You deserve our family's undying gratitude. And, you deserve God's love, His grace, and His peace. May you enjoy God's blessings always, and may you never, ever forget how much we love you.

Signed,
YOUR LOVING FAMILY

THOUGHTS ABOUT THANKSGIVING

It is always possible to be thankful for what is given rather than to complain about what is not given. One or the other becomes a habit of life.

ELISABETH ELLIOT

We ought to give thanks for all fortune: if it is good, because it is good, if bad, because it works in us patience, humility, and the contempt of this world along with the hope of our eternal country.

C. S. LEWIS

Praise and thank God for who He is and for what He has done for you.

BILLY GRAHAM

God has promised that if we harvest well with
the tools of thanksgiving, there will be seeds for
planting in the spring.

GLORIA GAITHER

Thanksgiving or complaining—these words express
two contrastive attitudes of the souls of God's
children in regard to His dealings with them.
The soul that gives thanks can find comfort
in everything; the soul that complains can
find comfort in nothing.

HANNAH WHITALL SMITH

God is in control, and therefore in everything
I can give thanks, not because of the situation,
but because of the One who directs
and rules over it.

KAY ARTHUR

God is worthy of our praise and is pleased
when we come before Him with thanksgiving.

SHIRLEY DOBSON

If you can't tell whether your glass is half-empty or
half-full, you don't need another glass;
what you need is better eyesight . . .
and a more thankful heart.

MARIE T. FREEMAN

Thanksgiving is good
but Thanksliving is better.

JIM GALLERY

The words "thank" and "think" come
from the same root word. If we would think more,
we would thank more.

WARREN WIERSBE

The act of thanksgiving is a demonstration of
the fact that you are going to trust and believe God.

KAY ARTHUR

Do you know that if at birth I had been able to
make one petition, it would have been that I should
be born blind? Because, when I get to heaven,
the first face that shall ever gladden my sight
will be that of my Savior!

FANNY CROSBY

It is only with gratitude that life becomes rich.

DIETRICH BONHOEFFER

A child of God should be a visible beatitude
for joy and a living doxology for gratitude.

C. H. SPURGEON

Contentment comes when we develop an attitude of
gratitude for the important things we *do* have in
our lives that we tend to take for granted if we have
our eyes staring longingly at our neighbor's stuff.

DAVE RAMSEY

Think of the blessings we so easily take for granted:
Life itself; preservation from danger; every bit of
health we enjoy; every hour of liberty; the ability to
see, to hear, to speak, to think, and to imagine
all this comes from the hand of God.

BILLY GRAHAM

For three years, I felt like all I did was pick up toys,
coordinate naps, and kiss boo-boos. But I began to
realize that there was a whole other level to my life
and that I'd never had a more important job:
I was teaching my children how to respond to God.

LISA WHELCHEL

A true mother is not merely a provider, housekeeper,
comforter, or companion. A true mother is primarily
and essentially a trainer.

RUTH BELL GRAHAM

God wants to make something beautiful of our lives;
our task—as God's children and
as our children's parents—is to let Him.

JIM GALLERY

I believe our primary task as parents is to train them
to constantly discover the God of life in
the big world by slowly, carefully, and progressively
broadening their boundaries.

BETH MOORE

WE PREVENT GOD
FROM GIVING US
THE GREAT SPIRITUAL
GIFTS HE HAS IN STORE
FOR US, BECAUSE
WE DO NOT GIVE THANKS
FOR DAILY GIFTS.

—

DIETRICH BONHOEFFER

MORE
VERSES TO
CONSIDER

GIFTS AND TALENTS

Now there are varieties of gifts, but the same Spirit.
And there are varieties of ministries, and the same Lord.

1 CORINTHIANS 12:4-5 NASB

God has given gifts to each of you from his great variety
of spiritual gifts. Manage them well so that
God's generosity can flow through you.

1 PETER 4:10 NLT

Do not neglect the spiritual gift that is within you . . . .

1 TIMOTHY 4:14 NASB

Every good gift and every perfect gift is from above,
and cometh down from the Father of lights.

JAMES 1:17 KJV

SEEKING GOD

Seek the LORD while he may be found;
call on him while he is near.

ISAIAH 55:6 NIV

You will seek me and find me when you seek me
with all your heart.

JEREMIAH 29:13 NIV

But seek first his kingdom and his righteousness,
and all these things will be given to you as well.

MATTHEW 6:33 NIV

If my people, who are called by my name,
will humble themselves and pray and seek my face and
turn from their wicked ways, then will I hear from
heaven and will forgive their sin and will heal their land.

2 CHRONICLES 7:14 NIV

PRIORITIES

*And I pray this: that your love will keep on growing
in knowledge and every kind of discernment,
so that you can determine what really matters
and can be pure and blameless in the day of Christ.*

PHILIPPIANS 1:9 HCSB

*He said to them all, "If anyone desires
to come after Me, let him deny himself,
and take up his cross daily, and follow Me.
For whoever desires to save his life will lose it,
but whoever loses his life for My sake will save it."*

LUKE 9:23-24 NKJV

*Let us fix our eyes on Jesus, the author and perfecter of
our faith, who for the joy set before him endured
the cross, scorning its shame, and sat down at
the right hand of the throne of God.*

HEBREWS 12:2 NIV

FIRST PAY ATTENTION TO ME, AND THEN RELAX. NOW YOU CAN TAKE IT EASY— YOU'RE IN GOOD HANDS.

—

PROVERBS 1:33 MSG